I0201305

The Church

and

The Bride

McDougal & Associates

Servants of Christ and Stewards of the
Mysteries of God

The Church

and

The Bride

Are They One and the Same?

by

Phyllis Harper Isenhart

THE CHURCH AND THE BRIDE

Published by:
McDougal & Associates
18896 Greenwell Springs Road
Greenwell Springs, LA 70739
www.thepublishedword.com

McDougal & Associates is dedicated to the spreading of the Gospel of Jesus Christ to as many people as possible in the shortest time possible.

ISBN 978-1-940461-50-2
Printed on demand in the US, the UK and Australia
For Worldwide Distribution

Dedication

I dedicate this book to my Redeemer and the one True Lover of My Soul, Jesus Christ. He is the One who found me in my fallen state and gave me new life. He is the One who, at the lowest point of my life, appeared to me and sang me a love song: *"With an Everlasting Love, I Will Love You."* When He had finished singing, He backed out through the same wall He had come in through, proving to me that He would never turn His back on me.

He is the One who has been with me through sickness, bringing me through thyroid cancer unscathed, as well as through many other sicknesses. He is the One who walked with me through the death of family members and loved ones, several of them back-to-back within just a few months of each other.

He was the One who inspired this writing, revealing His Word to me in ways that I had never before seen or heard before. I thank Him every day for His presence in my life and so dedicate this work to Him — Jesus Christ, the Author and Finisher of my faith.

Acknowledgments

There have been many, down through the years, who have played an integral part in my life and whom I would like to acknowledge at this time:

First, **my parents**, who taught me from an early age to follow Christ and trust Him in all things. Thank you, Mom and Dad, for living a godly life as an example for me to follow.

To **Beverly, Bill, Chris** and **Chuck, my four children**, what can I say, but you have been my reason to continue on when I actually feel like giving up. You have been such a source of encouragement. Each of you, as different as you are, is special and unique in your own way and have brought much joy to my life. To **my grandchildren** and one **great-grandchild**, I love you and thank you for being you.

And finally, I cannot leave out my church family, **Liberty Center International Church**, and **Pastor/ Apostle Edna Cavenaugh**. It has been such a delight to sit under your ministry for the last sixteen years. You have taught me so much, for which I am eternally gratefully.

I Will Love You with an Everlasting Love

"When you're walking through the valley, I'll lead you.
On the fatness of the land I'll feed you.
And a mansion up on high I'll leave you.
And the high places I will bring down.

All the mysterious of the Kingdom I'll show you.
And there'll come a time when the world won't know you.
But my Father and I will hold you.

And the high places I will bring down.

Chorus:
With and everlasting love I'll love you.
And when trials deepen sore, I'll prove you.
But there's nothing in this world that will hurt you.
And the high places I will bring down.

Contents

Let us be glad and rejoice, and give honour to him: for the marriage of the Lamb is come, and his wife hath made herself ready.   Revelation 19:7

Introduction

Who is this bride, the Bride of Christ? And where does she come from? These are questions that I began to ponder over in my mind after attending a teaching seminar on the Bride of Christ some years ago. From childhood I had always had the impression that these two — the Church and the Bride — were synonymous, in other words, one and the same. But was it true? As I began to read and study the Scriptures more thoroughly on this subject, I began to see things in a very different way.

The more I studied, the more it seemed to me as if the Church and the Bride were not necessarily the same. Then I began asking myself, "Well, if they are not one and the same, what is the distinguishing factor? And how can we tell one from the other?" It was what I felt the Lord showing me in response to these questions that eventually led to my writing this little book. This was important information, and it had to be shared.

The only reference materials I used in this study were the Bible (I used both the *King James Version* and the *New American Standard Version*), *Strong's Concordance* and *Vine's Expository Dictionary of New Testament Words*. God did the rest by His Spirit.

Now, some years later, I am happy to have the book professionally published, and my prayer is that the teaching that has blessed me so much will also bless many others.

Phyllis Harper Isenhart
Jacksonville, North Carolina

Chapter 1

Back to the Beginning

And the LORD God caused a deep sleep to fall upon Adam, and he slept: and he took one of his ribs, and closed up the flesh instead thereof; and the rib, which the LORD God had taken from man, made he a woman, and brought her unto the man. And Adam said, This is now bone of my bones, and flesh of my flesh: she shall be called Woman, because she was taken out of Man. Genesis 2:21-23

To start my search for understanding the Bride of Christ, I went back to the beginning, back to Creation, back to Genesis, back to the first marriage, the union of Adam and Eve. What I learned from the example of this, the first man and woman to be joined, was clear: Adam's bride was taken out of Adam's side, from his own body.

So, if Adam's bride was taken out of his body, what could be said for the Bride of Christ? Is this a valid comparison. Yes, for Jesus is referred to in Scripture as the second Adam or *"last Adam."*

I searched further, and this is what I found:

So also it is written, "The first man, Adam, became a living soul." The last Adam became a life-giving spirit.
1 Corinthians 15:45, NASB

And hath put all things under his feet, and gave him to be the head over all things to the church, which is his body, the fulness of him that filleth all in all. Ephesians 1:22-23

Now ye are the body of Christ, and members in particular.
1 Corinthians 12:27

It is clear from these passages that the Church is the Body of Christ. I think most of us agree on that point.

Malachi tells us that God does not change:

For I am the LORD, I change not. Malachi 3:6

Since God doesn't change, and since He took the first Adam's bride out of Adam's own body, I submit that He will also take the Bride of the second Adam (who is Christ), out of His Body.

As we have established, that Body is the Church. If this is true (and it is), then not all who are a part of the Church will be part of the Bride. It's like the proverbial saying: all Chryslers are cars, but not all cars are Chryslers. All Christians are part of the Church, but not all Christians are part of the Bride. To me, that was a revelation, and it led me to dig deeper to see what more I could find.

Chapter 2

What Is the Difference?

And it came to pass, as the camels had done drinking, that the man took a golden earring of half a shekel weight, and two bracelets for her hands of ten shekels weight of gold.

Genesis 24:22

If there is a difference between the Church and the Bride, and there clearly is, what is that difference? How can a person

23

know if he or she is part of the Bride? Here in our country, when a young man asks his girlfriend to marry him and she accepts, he usually presents her with an engagement ring. That ring is a sign, or symbol, of their engagement. This was the reason Abraham's servant, Eleazar, placed jewels on Rebekah, first as a sign that she was spoken for and then again, once she had agreed to become Isaac's wife.

Later, when Eleazar was re-telling the event, it is even more clear what his intentions were in this matter:

And I asked her, and said, Whose daughter art thou? And she said, the daughter of Bethuel, Nahor's son, whom Milcah bare unto him: and I put the earring upon her face, and the bracelets upon her hands. And I bowed down my head, and worshipped the Lord, and blessed the Lord God of my master Abraham, which had led me in the right way to take my master's brother's daughter unto his son.

Genesis 24:47-48

The jewels that were lavished upon Rebekah served as a

pledge, or seal, and as a witness to the rest of the world that she now belonged to Isaac and to none other.

But what does this mean to us today? What does Jesus give us that shows the world that we are His? He gives us what He termed *"the promise of the Father,"* and this is the gift of the Holy Spirit (Acts 1:4).

Some believe that this happens to us at salvation. I must admit that at one point in my life I thought the same thing. It is true that the Holy Spirit fills every new believer, but He does not baptize, or immerse, them in His power at that time. This is an important point, so let us examine the Scriptures carefully in this regard.

John described Jesus as telling His disciples:

> *Nevertheless I tell you the truth; It is expedient for you that I go away: for if I go not away, the Comforter will not come unto you; but if I depart, I will send him unto you.*
>
> John 16:7

This took place prior to the crucifixion. Later John described Jesus appearing to the disciples after the crucifixion and resurrection but before He ascended into Heaven. He also spoke something very important to them that day:

> *Then said Jesus to them again, Peace be unto you: as my Father hath sent me, even so send I you. And when he had said this, he breathed on them, and saith unto them, Receive ye the Holy Ghost.* John 20:21-22

This seems to be the moment when the disciples received salvation as we know it today. It comes through the Holy Spirit.

But remember that Jesus had not yet ascended to the Father.

Luke also recorded what Jesus called *"the promise of my Father"*:

And, behold, I send the promise of my Father upon you: but tarry ye in the city of Jerusalem, until ye be endued with power from on high. Luke 24:49

It is apparent from these passages that when Jesus breathed on the disciples (before His ascension) they received the Holy Spirit, but this was clearly not *"the promise of the Father"* that Jesus had spoken of. This promise would come only after He had left the earth and returned to the Father.

Luke recorded Jesus' important words to His disciples before He left them:

And, being assembled together with them, commanded them that they should not depart from Jerusalem, but wait for the promise of the Father, which, saith he, ye have heard of me. For John truly baptized with water; but ye shall be baptized with the Holy Ghost not many days hence.

Acts 1:4-5

Verse 8 of that same chapter is
so important to our understanding of God's gift to His beloved:

> *But ye shall receive power,*
> *after that the Holy Ghost is*
> *come upon you: and ye shall*
> *be witnesses unto me both in*
> *Jerusalem, and in all Judaea,*
> *and in Samaria, and unto the*
> *uttermost part of the earth.*
> Acts 1:8

It seems clear to me that *"the*
promise of the Father," the baptism in the Holy Spirit, is the
gift God give us that seals us as
belonging to Him.

Jesus kept His word, and the Spirit came just as He had promised:

And when the day of Pentecost was fully come, they were all with one accord in one place. And suddenly there came a sound from heaven as of a rushing mighty wind, and it filled all the house where they were sitting. And there appeared unto them cloven tongues like as of fire, and it sat upon each of them. And they were all filled with the Holy Ghost, and began to speak with other tongues, as the Spirit gave them utterance. Acts 2:1-4

This was the fulfillment of Jesus' promise, the baptism of the Holy Spirit, the seal of God's love upon His Beloved.

Chapter 3

Gaining Insight from the Parable of the Ten Virgins

Then shall the kingdom of heaven be likened unto ten virgins, which took their lamps, and went forth to meet the bridegroom. And five of them were wise, and five were foolish.   Matthew 25:1-2

Jesus told this important parable that we have come to call the Parable of the Ten Virgins. To my way of thinking, these virgins represent the members of the true Church. They were all going forth to meet the bridegroom, who we know is Jesus. They all had their lamps (our life is our lamp), and their lamps were filled with oil (which is symbolic of the Holy Spirit). And yet, as verse 2 indicates, five of them were *"foolish"* and verse 4 tells us why. They took no extra oil with them. They had only what had been in their vessels from the start. The other

36

virgins are called *"wise,"* and it is because they took extra oil with them, when the foolish did not.

While all ten of these virgins waited for the bridegroom (again representing Jesus), they became drowsy and slept. Doesn't that paint a vivid picture of the Church of our day? Then, at midnight, a shout was heard announcing the coming of the bridegroom. Paul gave us this beautiful picture of what that moment will be like:

For the Lord himself shall descend from heaven with

*a shout, with the voice of
the archangel, and with the
trump of God.*

1 Thessalonians 4:16

What a day that will be!

When the shout came at midnight, all ten of the virgins arose (a picture of the Rapture of the Church). Immediately they trimmed (or lighted) their lamps. It was then that the foolish virgins discovered that they were out of oil and began asking the five wise virgins for some of theirs. But you can't make it on someone else's oil. You need the Holy Spirit anointing for yourself. So you must get your own.

The sad ending of the story is that while the foolish virgins were out seeking more oil, the bridegroom came. And when they finally did arrive, it was too late. The groom had already taken his bride.

So what does all of this mean to us today? The only way to be sure that you don't run out of oil is to be *in* the oil. When you are being baptized, or immersed, in the Holy Spirit, your lamp is in the oil Himself, and you won't have to worry about running out or of missing Him. So you have to stay in the oil, or in the Spirit.

Paul encouraged the Corinthian believers with these words:

Now he which stablisheth us with you in Christ, and hath anointed us, is God; who hath also sealed us, and given the earnest of the Spirit in our hearts.

2 Corinthians 1:21-22

This word *earnest* means "a partial payment or deposit." The New International Version of the Bible says it like this:

Now it is God who makes both us and you stand firm in Christ. He anointed us, set his seal of ownership on us, and put his Spirit in our hearts as a deposit, guaranteeing what is to come.

Paul wrote to the Ephesian Church:

In whom ye also trusted, after that ye heard the word of truth, the gospel of your salvation: in whom also after that ye believed, ye were sealed with that holy Spirit of promise, which is the earnest of our inheritance until the redemption of the purchased possession, unto the praise of his glory.

Ephesians 1:13-14

Brothers and sisters, Jesus has given us the baptism in the Holy Spirit as an engagement ring!

Chapter 4

What Is the Baptism in the Holy Spirit?

And it shall come to pass afterward, that I will pour out my spirit upon all flesh; and your sons and your daughters shall prophesy, your old men shall dream dreams, your young men shall see visions: and also upon the servants and upon the handmaids in those days will I pour out my spirit. Joel 2:28-29

What then is this baptism in the Holy Spirit? What is its purpose and how do I get it? These are all important questions that require answers.

As a starting point, the prophet Isaiah, some four hundred years before Christ, spoke of this experience:

For with stammering lips and another tongue will he speak to this people. Isaiah 28:11

As noted in the theme verse for this chapter, Joel also prophesied of it. His prophecy was fulfilled on the Day of Pentecost:

And when the day of Pentecost was fully come, they were all with one accord in one place. And suddenly there came a sound from heaven as of a rushing mighty wind, and it filled all the house where they were sitting. And there appeared unto them cloven tongues like as of fire, and it sat upon each of them. And they were all filled with the Holy Ghost, and began to speak with other tongues, as the Spirit gave them utterance.   Acts 2:1-4

I have had people ask me, "Who has ever seen tongues of

fire sitting over people?" Let's examine these scriptures very carefully to see what actually happened that day.

As we noted earlier, Jesus, just before He ascended back to the Father, instructed the disciples to *"tarry,"* or wait, in Jerusalem until they were *"endued with power from on high"* (Luke 24:49. In obedience to Christ's command, the disciples were waiting in an upper room.

More than the original disciples were there waiting. The Scriptures show that there were actually one hundred and twenty of them in all (see Acts 1:15).

Another interesting things is that they were *"with one accord"* (verse 14). This simply means that their hearts and minds were on the same thing. They had gathered to praise God and seek His face for their future and that of the Church.

They had been waiting in this room now for ten days, ever since Jesus had been taken away. Then, very suddenly, something began to happen.

At first, what they noticed was a strange noise. It sounded to them like a very strong wind was blowing through the house. The sound of it filled all the rooms of the house, not just the one they had gathered in. There was no actual wind, just the sound of a wind.

Then something else happened. What appeared to be *"cloven tongues as of fire"* appeared, and *the Scriptures say "sat upon them."* What does that mean? The word that was translated as *cloven* here is the Greek word *diamerizo,* and it means "to partition throughly." This indicates that their tongues were moving in an unusual way, a way that reminded them of how flames of fire act.

As the disciples continued praising God, their tongue, or language, changed into one that was strange, or unknown, to them. This was the fulfillment of the prophecy of Isaiah:

For with stammering lips and another tongue will he speak to this people. To whom he said, This is the rest wherewith ye may cause the weary to rest; and this is the refreshing: yet they would not hear.

Isaiah 28:11-12

The Hebrew word translated to English as *stammering* comes

from the word *laag*, which means "to divide, by implication (as if imitating a foreigner); to speak unintelligibly," and the Hebrew word translated *another* is *acher*, which means "strange."

In Acts 2:4, the Greek word translated as *other* is *heteros*, which is also translated *strange*. What was happening here? These people were being baptized, or immersed, in the Holy Spirit. Now they not only had the Spirit in them; they were in the Spirit.

Some insist, "That was all well and good for them, but this experience is not for today."

But according to Acts 2:39, this experience is for us too. Peter declared:

> *For the promise is unto you, and to your children, and to all that are afar off, even as many as the Lord our God shall call.*

Those of us who have received this wonderful experience have known this truth for some time now. We just wish that many others could enjoy the benefits we are enjoying. There's nothing like it.

Chapter 5

What Is the Purpose of the Baptism in the Holy Spirit?

But ye shall receive power, after that the Holy Ghost is come upon you: and ye shall be witnesses unto me both in Jerusalem, and in all Judaea, and in Samaria, and unto the uttermost part of the earth.

Acts 1:8

This passage makes it clear. The purpose of the baptism in the Holy Spirit is to give us the power to live an overcoming life, so that others may see and believe. It gives us the power to work miracles, so that others may see and believe. It gives us the power, or authority, to heal the sick, so that others may see and believe.

This wonderful experience enables us to look temptation in the face and say "No!" It enables us to walk through the storms of life and still have peace, so that others may see and believe. It enable us to love those who are unlovable, so that they may know Jesus and believe. And I could go on. There is so much that the Holy Spirit baptism does for us that there can be no comparison made between our lives before and after having received this promise of the Father.

Chapter 6

How Do I Receive the Baptism in the Holy Spirit?

Now that we have examined what the baptism in the Holy Spirit is and what the purpose is, you may ask, "How do I get this baptism in the Holy Spirit?" I don't believe there is specific set of steps to follow to receive this baptism. However, I will say you have to truly believe it is real and have a heart's desire to receive everything God has for you.

On the Day of Pentecost, the one hundred twenty were gathered together in one accord, or with one purpose. That purpose was to worship God. Then this experience of the baptism in the Holy Spirit came to them.

I can only relate what happened to me when I received the baptism in the Holy Spirit. I surrendered to Christ in March of 1979 and had a very dynamic encounter with Jesus that day. For the next couple of months,

I was like a sponge. I could not get enough of God. There was so much to learn, and I felt like I couldn't learn it all quickly enough.

Then, in May of 1979, during an altar call, I went to the front of the church and just started thanking and blessing God for who He was and for what He had done. (I must add that my praise and worship was not a quiet, thinking in the mind, but rather an audible, out loud expression of my gratitude and love for Him.) In the course of that worship, Jesus baptized me in His Holy Spirit, and my language began to change into a language I had never spoken or even heard before.

This was a physical sign to me that something had happened, but what transpired within my spirit was so much more. Words cannot express what began to happen there. Now there was a peace like I had never known before, there was joy unspeakable and a reassurance that the Spirit would always be with me. Afterward, as I read and studied the Bible, it began to come alive to me, and I had an understanding and revelation of it like I had never known before.

Since that Sunday evening in May 1979, the Holy Spirit has been with me through good times and bad. He has been to me a Healer, a Comforter, a Teacher and a Guide. He is my everything.

As I said, there is no set-in-stone way to receive this baptism in the Holy Spirit. It is Jesus who determines how He does it. I know a pastor who pulled in behind a Dairy Queen and received the baptism while sitting in his car. I've known others who received it at home during their personal prayer time.

I do believe the two requirements are: first, to believe that it is real and, second, to desire it and ask for it with a pure heart.

You may not receive the Holy Spirit baptism the first time you ask God for it, but don't give up. If you are persistent, He will do this for you.

Chapter 7

What About Speaking in Tongues?

And these signs shall follow them that believe; In my name shall they cast out devils; they shall speak with new tongues.

Mark 16:17

And they were all filled with the Holy Ghost, and began to speak with other tongues, as

the Spirit gave them utterance.
Acts 2:4

Cretes and Arabians, we do hear them speak in our tongues the wonderful works of God.
Acts 2:11

For they heard them speak with tongues, and magnify God.
Acts 10:46

I would that ye all spake with tongues. 1 Corinthians 14:5

I thank my God, I speak with tongues more than ye all.
1 Corinthians 14:18

Whenever the baptism in the Holy Spirit is mentioned, the next question people ask is "what about speaking in tongues?" Sadly, many get hung up on this point.

Speaking in other (or strange or unknown) tongues (they all mean the same) is the initial, physical evidence of the baptism in the Holy Spirit. There will be other evidences also, but this is the first.

I would rather not spend too much time here examining this issue of speaking in tongues. Let me just say that there are some very valid uses for this gift. But the purpose of the baptism in the Holy Spirit is not just so that we can speak in tongues. Again, it is to give us the power and authority to be Christ's witnesses. Tongues is merely a sign that we have this power. Now, that said, let's get back to the subject of the Bride.

Chapter 8

When Will the Bride Be Taken Out of the Church?

Let not your heart be troubled: ye believe in God, believe also in me. In my Father's house are many mansions: if it were not so, I would have told you. I go to prepare a place for you. And if I go and prepare a place for you, I will come again, and receive you unto myself; that where I am, there ye may be also. John 14:1-3

This is Jesus' promise to return for us. The angels who appeared at His ascension confirmed this promise:

And while they looked stedfastly toward heaven as he went up, behold, two men stood by them in white apparel; which also said, Ye men of Galilee, why stand ye gazing up into heaven? this same Jesus, which is taken up from you into heaven, shall so come in like manner as ye have seen him go into heaven.   Acts 1:10-11

Paul described the catching away of the Body of Christ to meet Him in the clouds:

For the Lord himself shall descend from heaven with a shout, with the voice of the archangel, and with the trump of God: and the dead in Christ shall rise first: then we which are alive and remain shall be caught up together with them in the clouds, to meet the Lord in the air: and so shall we ever be with the Lord.
            1 Thessalonians 4:16-17

This event is what much of the church world has come to call the Rapture of the Church. Since the Church is Christ's Body, it is His whole Body that will be caught away to be with Him. The general consensus is that this will take place just prior to the Tribulation. It will be at this time that the Father will present the Bride to the Groom, and the marriage will take place.

After the wedding, there will be a reception. This is what the Bible calls the Marriage Supper of the Lamb, and all believers are invited. On that day, will you be an observer? Or are you determined to be part of the Bride. I can't speak for you, but I intend to be part of the Bride on that glorious day.

About the Author

Phyllis Harper Isenhart was born November 4, 1947 in eastern North Carolina, the third of four children born to Saint Elmo and Nancy Willis Harper. Yes, although he went by Elmo, Saint was her father's given first name at birth. He was a Free Will Baptist preacher and pastor, so from the time she was born, she was carried to church. In June of 1958, she accepted Christ as her personal Savior and was baptized in water.

Phyllis graduated high school and went on to college for a while. For the next ten years, however, she did her own thing. In 1970 she married a marine, and together they had four children. By 1984, she found herself in a legal separation, which finally ended in divorce in 1996.

Phyllis went to church off and on but was never happy with the result. Then, in March of 1978, while the family was living in Beaufort, South Carolina, her two older children began urging her to go to church with them. They had been riding a church bus for about a year and one particular Sunday if they brought a visitor with them, they would get to fish a gift out of a pool. For several weeks, they begged her to go, until she finally relented and said okay.

Phyllis was not aware of the fact that this was the very same church she had attended a couple of years before and vowed never to go back to. As it turned out, it was the same church building, but it was not the same church. They had changed pastors in the meantime. That Sunday became her new spiritual birthday. She surrendered her life to Christ and decided to follow Him all the days of her life.

Now Phyllis was like a sponge. She simply could not get enough of God. That May she was baptized in the Holy Ghost, and for the next three years, she sat under the teaching of Rev. Gaylon and Barbara Benton, who became her mentors and very dear friends.

In December of 1981, Phyllis' husband was transferred to Camp Lejeune,

North Carolina, and there she was introduced to an Assembly of God church in Jacksonville, which she began to attend. It was during this time that her marriage began to fall apart, and her whole world seemed to fall apart with it. One day, while she was at her very lowest point, she was sitting on her couch with her head in her hands, crying out to God. Suddenly, Jesus appeared before her and sang her a love song:

*When you are walking through the valley, I'll lead you.
On the fatness of the land, I will feed you.*

75

After Jesus finished singing this song, He backed out through the same wall He had come in through, proving to Phyllis that He would never ever turn His back on her. That made such an impact on her life that she was never the same again. She knew from that day forward that there was nothing she could not get through and that the Lord would be right beside her.

He was there with her in 2000, when her husband passed away. He was there with her in 2003, when she laid her mother to rest. He was there in 2013 when, in the course of three months, she lost a brother, a brother-in-law and two sisters-in-law. And He kept her through it all.

It has been Jesus' everlasting love that has propelled Phyllis onward, to press toward the mark of the high calling in Christ Jesus. It is in Him that she lives and moves and has her being.

You may contact the author at:

Phyllis Isenhart
1861 Pony Farm Road, Lot 4
Jacksonville, NC 28540

or

pisenhart@twc.com

www.ingramcontent.com/pod-product-compliance
Lightning Source LLC
Chambersburg PA
CBHW021218020426
42331CB00003B/357